Sue & Terry,

Happy 39th wedding anniversary. Thanks for sharing your day with Door County Trolley.

John Bauer

D0856090

Door County

Trolley

"I have been meeting with John for the last 10 years almost every morning. His memory is phenomenal. One time I asked him who made an unassisted triple play, and he responded with the name of the player, game and date. Many more conversations on his recollection of baseball statistics are of a similar nature. Once John starts talking, get out of the way, he's on a roll. At that point, the only difference between John and our local radio stations is you can turn off the radio!"

—**Dan Austad,** retired owner *Door County Hardware* and former Door County Board Chairman

"John Berns is unparalleled in his love and respect for the game of baseball, its traditions and legendary characters. He keeps his friends entertained with his stories and former player quotes. One of John's many gifts is the ability to coach and positively influence the young men on his team. His primary tools include exceptional baseball acumen, humor, and his own life lessons. I truly respect John for the person he is: devotion to his family, friends, players and mankind in general."

—**Mike Barry,** retired Director of Institutional Support, *UW Green Bay*

"Besides being a good friend of mine, John Berns is a great family man, an individual respected in the community, and a great authority on sports, particularly the sport of baseball. His memories as a player and coach are very special."

—**Rev. Tony Birdsall,** retired Catholic priest

"Bernsy wrote a book? Really? I'm not sure he has a signed high school diploma!"

—**Bill Aune,** retired teacher and coach

9 INNINGS OF MEMORIES AND HEROES

9 Innings of Memories and Heroes

Copyright © 2020 *John Berns*

ISBN: 9781735346915

A Publication of Tall Pine Books

|| *tallpinebooks.com*

*Printed in the United States of America

9 INNINGS OF MEMORIES AND HEROES

JOHN BERNS

WITH TOM ROY

TALL PINE
BOOKS

To my wife, Kris. You have been with me on most of the steps (and missteps) of my baseball journey.

After forty-nine years of marriage, it has become crystal clear that you will always be my best teammate. You are the most caring and loving person I will ever meet.

To our special needs son, Brian. You never were able to play baseball. However, you have proved to be our inspiration and hero. Your ability to navigate over, under, and around all the obstacles which have been placed in front of you, shows how very special you really are.

To our daughter, Amy. You were on the first two teams I ever coached. Those memories will forever be held close to my heart. I will always call you my "Little Miss Muffet." We are so very blessed that two beautiful little girls call you "Mommy" – our granddaughters Elsa and Ada.

I love each of you more than you could imagine.

CONTENTS

FOREWORD

This is a book about baseball, memories, and heroes.

I had the privilege of meeting John Berns a few years ago when he was guiding a tour of one of the historic lighthouses of Door County. He noticed I was wearing a baseball shirt and I discovered he was the head baseball coach at Sturgeon Bay High School.

Coach Berns has a keen interest in history, including local Door County history and baseball history, especially the Milwaukee Braves. He is a one-of-a-kind, and this is his 'legacy book' as he narrates events that framed and directed his life.

John is a natural storyteller, with the ability to draw pictures with words that will take you back to a place in your own life. Teams, individuals, and stories may differ, but his memories of youth baseball, influencers and heroes will resonate.

Then you, the reader, will have the opportunity to write your own story! John will help you capture your personal memories with a series of questions that will lead you to write out your own legacy—a treasure for those you love for years to come.

Get ready to dream and reminisce about days gone by!

—**Tom Roy**, Author and Founder of *UPI*
and *Shepherd Coach Network*

PREFACE

Included within the dictionary definition of **inning** is the following: *An opportunity for an activity: a turn.*

Within this book you will learn of the opportunities and activities from some of the innings in my life.

You will then be provided with "a turn" at the end of each inning.

The following is included in the dictionary definition of **memory**: *The retaining and recalling of past experience; the act or instance of remembrance.* Your memories allow you to revisit certain special times and places. It can result in a brilliant sun breaking through on your cloudiest of days. A good memory is something which will last a lifetime. You can draw on it anytime you choose.

Heroes are often mythological or legendary figures. Those descriptions DO NOT fit my definition of hero. My definition of hero includes caring fathers, gifted announcers, and dedicated coaches. Also included in this group are people who have passed in and out of my life for a brief moment, but who left behind a special memory. These select people will always be my heroes!

The Best Picture nominees for 1990 were Dead Poets Society, My Left Foot, Driving Miss Daisy, and Field Of Dreams. My belief was that Field of Dreams would be the runaway winner. However, Driving Miss Daisy ran away with the Oscar. Sometime after the award presentation, Field of Dreams director Phil Alden Robinson shared a moving story. He had received a call from a young man who had been estranged from his father for decades.

After attending Robinson's film that man called his father, and that shattered relationship was saved. The director stated that winning the Best Picture award would have been special, but that phone call was his Oscar! My wishes and hopes are that people reading this book will reconnect with some special someone who is no longer a part of their lives. If but one instance of that occurs, those many hours devoted to this project will have proven to be time well spent.

1ST INNING - DAD

Les Berns (Dad) with son, Tom.

IT'S A NO CLOUD IN THE SKY DAY IN SISTER BAY, ON A SPRING Saturday morning in 1957. Friends of mine are zooming past on their bicycles heading to the parks and beaches, but not me. This eight-year-old has his rear end pasted to the garage door of his family's home with tennis balls rocketing at him. Dad is the head rocket launcher, certainly throwing at major league speed as the balls bounce 2-3 feet in front of my trusty Billy Loes autographed baseball glove. Dad's message is simple, "Johnny, don't let the ball hit the garage door!" Dad knows that I have recently discovered this amazing game called baseball, and he is encouraging my interest. My favorite team is the Milwaukee Braves. Little do I know that within a month, a mere 190-mile trip in the family car will transport me to a life-changing new world.

Tom Berns batting with Coach Berns (John) observing.

Sunday, June 30, 1957 – Pittsburgh Pirates vs. Milwaukee Braves at Milwaukee County Stadium. Dad, brother Tom, and yours truly are part of a crowd of 36,283 attending a doubleheader – you got it, two games for the price of one, never to be seen again. It's only the bottom of the first inning, but Hank Aaron gets the crowd to rise as one by blasting a drive over the center field fence for a 1-0 Braves lead. An exciting game finds the score tied 2-2 in the bottom of the eighth inning.

The unpardonable lead-off walk to Eddie Mathews is followed by four singles and an error, and by the time the smoke clears the Braves lead 7-2. A ninth inning Pirates rally makes the final score 7-4. A thrilling game, but game two was about to provide a once-in-a-lifetime experience that would stay with me forever.

Time for Hank Aaron to strike again, as his fourth inning shot into the left field bleachers gave the Braves a 1-0 lead which would last until the top of the eighth. A bases clearing double by

Bill Mazeroski (about to make an indelible mark on baseball history in the 1960 World Series) produced a 4-1 Pittsburgh lead. An Aaron single in the bottom of the eighth closed the lead to 4-2, but Milwaukee still trailed by two runs in the bottom of the ninth with two out, and Frank Torre on base. However, the drive back to Sister Bay was delayed when Felix Mantilla planted a drive into the left field bleachers to square the account at 4. UNBELIEVABLE! Now we would be treated to extra innings.

Right when this eight-year-old thought it couldn't get any better – it got better! After the "bad guys" took a 5-4 lead in the top of the thirteenth, two future hall-of-famers would take care of business. Aaron led off with a single, and then lightning struck for the second time in the same game. Eddie Mathews deposited a drive into the bleachers in left-center field for an improbable 6-5 Braves victory. We had seen a "walk-off home run" before there was such a term as a "walk-off home run". The game of baseball now had a grip on me that thankfully would never allow me to break free.

Once again, Dad played a starring role at the end of the first inning of my baseball life. Even during summer vacation, Braves night games finished a trifle late for me to listen to the full game on my transistor radio. However, problem solved as follows: Each weekday morning on CBS television, there was a fifteen-minute news program from 6:45-7:00 am. The show, which ran from 1957-1961 was titled "Richard C. Hottelet with the News." Hottelet, a famous World War II reporter, provided all the previous night's baseball scores at about 6:55 am, Monday through Friday each week.

Dad religiously watched and recorded the scores for his son John. His notes would be placed on my spot at the kitchen table before Dad headed to Berns Brothers Lumber Company each day. I lived for those early morning scores, and if the note read something like Braves 5 Dodgers 4, my day had gotten off to a great start. Thanks, Dad.

NOW IT IS YOUR TURN!

On the pages that follow, write out your fondest memories of being a youngster.

1. What are your fondest memories of your dad or another leader in your life?

_____

_____

_____

_____

_____

_____

2. Share your earliest memories of attending baseball games (or any sporting event), both local and professional.

_____

_____

_____

_____

_____

_____

3. What activities caught your attention at the ages of 8-10?

_____

_____

_____

_____

_____

_____

4. Do you have a favorite location that was your "sweet spot" as a youngster?

_____

_____

_____

_____

_____

_____

2ND INNING - EARL GILLESPIE

SEPTEMBER 23, 1957

		1	2	3	4	5	6	7	8	9	10	11	R	H	E
	St. Louis Cardinals	0	0	0	0	0	2	0	0	0	0	0	2	9	3
	Milwaukee Braves	0	1	0	0	0	0	1	0	0	0	2	4	14	0

WP: Gene Conley (9-9) • LP: Billy Muffett (3-2)
Winning Run scored with 2 outs

OCTOBER 10,1957

		1	2	3	4	5	6	7	8	9	R	H	E
	Milwaukee Braves	0	0	4	0	0	0	0	1	0	5	9	1
	New York Yankees	0	0	0	0	0	0	0	0	0	0	7	3

WP: Lew Burdette (3-0) • LP: Don Larsen (1-1)

I FONDLY RECALL THE START TO ALL MILWAUKEE BRAVES HOME games in my formative baseball years. A distinct and unwavering voice would proclaim the following through my radio, "With Marvin Moran at the microphone, and Jane Jarvis at the organ, ladies and gentlemen, our national anthem." That distinct voice belonged to Earl Gillespie, the Braves radio play-by-play announcer from 1953-1963. Gillespie's knowledge of the game, welcoming voice, and announcing style was my main connection to baseball as I fell in love with the game in my youth. Earl made me feel like I was his friend, and he was simply describing the game action in great detail as I sat next to him. Along with his announcing partner, Blaine Walsh, he took me from being an excited youngster wanting to learn and understand baseball, to a teenager beginning to digest the subtleties and nuances of this beautiful game.

Gillespie always kept the broadcasts lively and entertaining. One would expect nothing less from a man nicknamed "Lippy" and "Gabby" by his minor league teammates because of his non-stop chatter. Dead air would not be a problem with Earl Gillespie in the booth!

I can still listen to my announcing hero any day I choose. The Milwaukee Braves released a vinyl record in 1962 which captured the radio broadcast highlights of the franchise from 1953-1961. A copy of "Go Get 'Em Braves" is an amazing compilation of achievements by those magical teams. Here are two of my favorite Milwaukee Braves moments captured forever by the voice and style of Earl Gillespie:

On September 23, 1957, Gillespie described the Braves winning the National League pennant this way: "The pitch to Henry Aaron. A swing and a drive back into center field!

Going back towards the wall! It's back at that fence . . . and is it caught or not? It's a home run! The Braves are the champions of the National League! Henry Aaron has just hit his forty-third home run of the year!"

On October 10, 1957, here is Gillespie's description of the Braves' World Series win: "The outfield around to the left. McDougald is at third, Coleman at second. Tommy Byrne is the base runner at first. Hank Aaron is pulled around in left-center field. A breeze is blowing across from left to right. Burdette's pitch. Swung on, lined, grabbed by Mathews who steps on third . . . and the World Series is over, and the Milwaukee Braves are the new world champions of baseball!"

A few additional notes regarding Mr. Gillespie: His outgoing style often had him finishing the description of a dramatic play with "Holy cow!" A distinguished broadcasting career also found him announcing games for the Green Bay Packers, Milwaukee Hawks, Wisconsin Badgers, and Marquette Warriors. His excellent career was recognized with his induction into the Wisconsin Athletic Hall of Fame in 2001.

Because of Gillespie's skill set, I was able to "see' Milwaukee Braves games on the radio!

YOUR TURN!

1. Who was your favorite celebrity as a youngster?

_____

_____

_____

_____

_____

_____

2. What captivated you during your teen years?

_____

_____

_____

_____

_____

_____

3. Who are some of the radio or TV announcers you remember from your youth? What are your fondest memories? What made them memorable?

_____

_____

_____

_____

_____

_____

4. Were there any famous personalities who had signature punch lines that became part of your vocabulary or memories?

_____

_____

_____

_____

_____

_____

3RD INNING - JOHN CURRAN

1960 Sturgeon Bay Little League Champions — Ships

(Front row from left) Greg Stephan, Steve Walker, Dick Spaete, Mike Olesen, Jerry MacMillin, Phil Spaeth, Tom Long; (Back row from left) Coach John Curran, Dick Haines, John Berns, Dick Smith, Barry DeMarb, Bud Schopf, Tom Ahrens, Mike Propsom, Assistant Coach Joe Morrow.

OUR FAMILY MOVED TO STURGEON BAY IN AUGUST OF 1959. IN September, brother Tom and I began school at Corpus

Christi Catholic Grade School ("Bless me Father, for I have sinned"). I was thrilled to discover that many of the boys in my fifth and sixth grade classroom also loved baseball. That spring brought the opportunity to try out for the Sturgeon Bay Little League. There were six teams in the league, and I was friends with boys on five of those teams. So which team drafts John Berns? The Ships: the only team which I was familiar with NONE of the players! Oh, well. Time to make some new friends.

1961 Sturgeon Bay Little League Co-Champions - Lake to Lake

That summer I became acquainted with a man named John Curran. John had a successful career as a civilian employee working for the United States Department of the Navy. He also spent time as the Park and Recreation Director for the city of Sturgeon Bay. However, I believe his true calling in life was to be a baseball coach, and lucky for me, my Little League coach. He was a short, stocky guy who always had his pants cuffs slightly wedged under the heels of his shoes.

Although his fashion style may have been below average, his coaching style was excellent. John Curran taught me how to work the count, only swing at strikes, bunt, and take extra bases - "small ball" at its finest. Our pitchers threw strikes, and defensive play was emphasized more than offense. Not surprisingly, this style of play resulted in the Ships winning the league title in 1960. That season the entire starting infield on the Sturgeon Bay Little League All-Star Team was from the same team . . . the Ships. It has never happened again!

One of the magic moments in my life occurred that summer. I was taking my two-mile bike ride home after an exciting 6-5 win over Stoneman's Funeral Home. As I rode down 3rd Avenue, Sturgeon Bay's main street, there stood John Curran and two other legendary youth coaches munching away at a curb-side popcorn stand. I was spell-bound as I listened to them evaluate our 6-5 victory, breaking down each inning play-by-play, and if necessary, pitch-by-pitch.

Then the wisdom came from the mouth of my coach. In talking about the value of having youngsters engaged in positive activities, he stated, "I would much rather have a kid at the ballpark trying to steal third base, than down on 3rd Avenue trying to steal everything." I cannot begin to explain what an impression those words made on an eleven year-old boy. At that moment, I determined that someday I wanted to be a baseball coach. A mere thirty-four years later I was hired to coach high school baseball in my home county. In 1996 John Curran was inducted into the Door County Baseball Hall of Fame. Of the hundreds of players he coached, and the countless other friends of John, he chose me to present him for induction. How special!

John had moved to Watertown, WI when he passed away on September 11, 2003. A memorial service was held in Sturgeon Bay on September 17th. I could not attend because of a prior commitment. That commitment involved six middle-aged guys spending an afternoon at Wrigley Field, watching Kerry Wood toss a 4-hit shutout at the NY Mets. I'm certain my coach would have approved of my choice on that particular day.

JOHN CURRAN IS 'PINNED' with a booster but-ton by Lee Berns in a mock ceremony after Curran was named commissioner and Berns president of the Bay Little League Tuesday night. Other new league officers watch. Left to right are Richard Bosman, treasurer; Berns; Curran; Bill Tong, vice president; and Don Olsen, secretary. —Advocate

HIGHLIGHTS OF THE Little League's opening day program are shown here. The top picture shows League President Les Berns presenting a baseball to guest of honor Keith Bink. Lower photo shows presentation of the George Fax Memorial trophy to managers of last year's three co-championship teams, left to right Curley Paul of Rotary, Ken Schreve of Kiwanis and Joe Morrow and John Curran of Lake to Lake. Curran is now league commissioner. —Harmann

YOUR TURN!

1. Describe all the relocations your family made when you were a child.

_____

_____

_____

_____

_____

_____

2. Who were some of your best friends prior to high school?

_____

_____

_____

_____

_____

_____

3. Who, other than a family member, had great influence in your life? Explain why.

_____

_____

_____

_____

_____

4. Explain your feelings when any of your close friends passed away.

_____

_____

_____

_____

_____

5. Name some of the values passed down to you by persons of influence in your life.

_____

_____

4TH INNING - LEON SCHRAM

IN LATE JUNE OF 1961 MY LITTLE LEAGUE COACH WAS CALLED out of town on business. John Curran informed our squad that Leon Schram would be replacing him for one game. I had no way of knowing that our replacement coach was about to provide me with a lifelong memory.

The 1968 obituary of Leon Schram included the following information: Member of the Holy Name Society of St. Joseph Catholic Church; member of American Legion Post 72; past Door County Civil Defense Director; employed at Peterson Builders, Inc. (PBI). It went on to say that he had served six years active duty during World War II. His survivors included his wife, four children, eight grandchildren, and two sisters. No information was provided indicating what a kind and thoughtful leader he had been. I will attempt to provide such information.

When the inaugural season for Sturgeon Bay Little League kicked off in 1953, Leon Schram volunteered to be an umpire. He later became coach of the Bushman's Travelers team, leading them to three consecutive championships, retiring from coaching after the 1959 title had been safely tucked away. Schram named one of his twelve-year-old stars to serve as coach in the final game of that season. Can you imagine that thrill? That impressionable boy later went on to manage for many years in the adult Door County League, and was instrumental in the formation of the Door County Baseball Hall of Fame.

In the spring of 1967, a graduating high school girl was hired to work in Schram's office at PBI. Although one had to work two weeks before receiving a first paycheck, at the end of week one that cute blonde found a dime taped to her windshield with the attached note: "Every Friday is payday at PBI." That young girl later told me that Mr. Schram once paid for a full tank of gas for '66 Chevy Malibu. By the way, I have now been married to that cute blonde for forty-nine years!

Ironically, the one game I played for Leon Schram was against his former Bushman's Travelers team. I played shortstop that day, and Coach Schram pulled me off to the side for some pre-game instruction. He told me that as the shortstop I had to provide leadership. I was to be vocal on pop-ups, covering bases, and communicating the situation to my teammates. No matter what occurred, I was to keep a cool head as the leader. He then said, "The only time your head should be down is when you are looking a ground ball into your glove." I am still using those words sixty years later.

I am certain that in addition to these brief stories, there are countless other examples of this man creating positive memories for young people. It is noteworthy that each year the Door County League baseball champion is awarded the Leon Schram Memorial Trophy.

Bart Starr once said he wished that every player could have played at least one game for Coach Lombardi. John Berns said he wished that every player could have played at least one game for Coach Schram.

YOUR TURN!

1. Is there someone who briefly entered your life, but left a lasting impression? Who was that person, and what did they say or do?

_____

_____

_____

_____

_____

_____

2. Write out the situations involved in the initial meeting of your spouse and any other stories about your dating and marriage.

_____

_____

_____

_____

_____

_____

3. What would you want written in your obituary?

_____

_____

_____

_____

_____

4. Are there any wise sayings that are now part of your normal understanding about life?

_____

_____

_____

_____

_____

5TH INNING - JOHN KETTENHOFEN

HIGH SCHOOL BASEBALL WAS A JOY IN THE SPRING OF 1964. As a freshman, I pitched two complete games with the varsity team, a 5-1 victory and a 3-0 loss, earning my first varsity letter at Southern Door. Summer baseball was even better in the 13-15-year-old Stars of Tomorrow League. Our team went undefeated, I tossed two no-hitters, and led the league with a .577 batting average.

Then my social life got a boost when as a 15-year-old, I met an engaging 14-year-old at the Door County Fair. Thankfully, she liked "older men" and the two of us became romantically linked for the entire next school year.

The only "negative" about that summer was my forty-five to fifty hour a week job at Berns Brothers Lumber Company, where my brother Tom and I were introduced to "favoritism in reverse." Every "lousy" job seemed to be given to the younger Berns brothers, the least favorite being unloading freight cars coming by rail from Chicago.

Here are the "lowlights" –

> 1. lumber wedged like pretzels at the top of a steamy freight car;
> 2. an endless supply of ½ inch thick, 4 x 8 foot layers of sheetrock at about 57 pounds per sheet;
> 3. a generous amount of shingles at 235 pounds per square (almost 80 pounds per bundle);
> 4. a rail car filled with 94-pound bags of Portland Cement (my personal favorite).

The valuable lesson learned was that I wanted little (or nothing) to do with manual labor for the balance of my life. Now for that special moment that brought me my fifth inning.

Our Stars of Tomorrow League season began with a two-inning practice game in early June. Prior to that game, the players walked around town selling $1 booster buttons. My catcher, George Viste and I headed straight to Memorial Drive, a beautiful Sturgeon Bay waterfront area.

Our sales were excellent in this "high rent" neighborhood. I'm not certain if George or yours truly suggested targeting Memorial Drive, but I can give you an educated guess. When we graduated in 1967, George graduated in the top five of our class, and I did not!

Now to the game. Everybody got to bat once. When my turn came, I hit a line drive into the left-center field gap for a sure double, but I decided to try for a triple. The throw beat me to third, but a very good hook slide to the home-plate side of the bag had me in safely. At the end of the game an elderly gentleman approached me to comment on my triple. He said, "That might end up being the best play that I will see this season." WOW – a complete stranger strolling up to a wide-eyed fifteen-year-old with those kind words.

I later learned that I had just met John Kettenhofen, at that time an eighty-year-old huge baseball fan. Mr. Kettenhofen had lost his wife twelve years earlier, and I soon discovered that he enjoyed spending the majority of his summer evenings at Door County baseball fields.

Throughout the summers of 1966 and 1967 I saw John in the stands at all of our Sturgeon Bay American Legion baseball home games. When he passed away in August of 1971 his obituary indicated he was survived by a daughter and two grandchildren. What I want to survive is the understanding of how a few kind and inspirational words have the power to tie multiple generations together. The same type of words I heard from John Kettenhofen.

YOUR TURN!

1. List all the jobs you have had over the years and what those jobs entailed.

_____

_____

_____

_____

_____

2. List some of your favorite relatives and what you liked best about each.

_____

_____

_____

_____

_____

_____

3. Can you remember any special people in your life who gave you that word of encouragement that made your day, year, life?

_____

_____

_____

_____

_____

_____

4. Drop a note to those special people listed above. If they are deceased, write or tell one of their loved ones what that person meant to you.

_____

_____

_____

_____

_____

_____

5. Who is in your life that could use a call, a cup of coffee or a kind word? You can make a difference!

_____

_____

_____

_____

_____

_____

6TH INNING - AL BREITLOW

ROW THREE: Reg Vandertie, manager; David Dahms, John Berns, Sam Malcore, Dennis Haskell, Roger Kipp, Bob Kreft, Mr. Brietlow, coach. ROW TWO: Jim Vogel, George Viste, Dennis Ullman, Larry Krueger, Lee Petrina, Mike Schmelzer. ROW ONE: Larry Dahms, Dave Columbo, Ron Vandertie, Herman Delfosse, Dave Sell, Dick Haines.

Southern Door's first ever conference baseball championship - 1965.

THE FIRST TIME I SAW MY HIGH SCHOOL BASEBALL COACH WALK into practice wearing his college letter jacket, I was guilty of one of the "7 Deadly Sins" - Envy. That letter "P" on his UW-Platteville jacket had been earned as a three-letter winner in football. Al Breitlow had also earned fifteen letters at Casco High School (four football, four basketball, four baseball, and three track), in between his numerous duties on the family farm in Rio Creek. He credits his high school baseball coach as being a mentor.

Gordy Goebel had played some professional baseball as a 5'8" first baseman, and according to Casco catcher Al Breitlow, he could still rifle the ball from first base to home plate. A second major influence was his agriculture teacher, Chet Majeski. Majeski had received his bachelor's degree from UW-Platteville, and was later inducted into that school's Athletic Hall of Fame. It was Majeski who convinced Breitlow that enrolling in college might provide an opportunity for a career away from the farm in Rio Creek. That it did!

Coach Breitlow and I crossed paths at Southern Door High School in the 1960's. He was my junior varsity basketball coach for two years, varsity baseball coach for four years, and varsity football coach for one year. We went 18-2 to win consecutive JV titles in basketball, and in 1965 won the first ever conference baseball title at Southern Door.

When Breitlow became head football coach in the fall of 1965, he talked me out of study hall and onto the football field. I was content as a starting wide receiver, but I became the starting varsity quarterback when our starting QB was sidelined with a season-ending injury in game one. History was made as John Berns helped lead Southern Door to a Peninsula Conference Co-championship. Now for Paul Harvey, and "The rest of the story."

There were six teams in the conference, with one team going 0-5, and the other five teams all finishing at 3-2. The impossible had occurred – a five-way tie for the title in a six team league. All five teams won a conference co-championship trophy in 1965!

My "fondest" memories of Coach Breitlow include him standing on my stomach while I was doing leg raises in the gym, having me run countless miles prior to pitching assignments, and then when I did pitch, hearing him say, "Go as hard as you can, for as long as you can." I am happy to share that we have maintained contact over these many years, and I was thrilled to be invited to Coach Breitlow's 80th birthday party in the summer of 2018.

I was blessed to have a caring and dedicated coach like Al Breitlow. This inning now concludes with a copy of a letter I received in the fall of 1993:

LOMBARDI MIDDLE SCHOOL
1520 South Point Road, Green Bay, WI 54313
(414) 492-2625

NANCY M. CROY, Principal
AL BREITLOW, Assistant Principal
JIM MEYERS, Assistant Principal

September 23, 1993

John,

Congratulations on your appointment as Head Baseball Coach at
Sevastopol High School!

I know that you will do a fine job. Your interest, desire and concerns
for kids is to be complimented. We need more persons like you in the
coaching profession.

Good luck and have a great season!

Sportingly yours,

Al Breitlow

That letter will still be in my possession the day I depart
this planet!

YOUR TURN!

1. What are your honest opinions about your high school coaches...if you played sports or not?

_____

_____

_____

_____

_____

2. Do you have contact with any of your high school teachers or coaches?

_____

_____

_____

_____

_____

3. What are your favorite high school memories?

_____

_____

_____

_____

_____

4. Do you have any notes, emails, texts or letters that you treasure? Please share them here.

_____

_____

_____

_____

_____

5. If you could write one letter to a former coach or teacher, who would it be, and what would you say?

_____

_____

_____

7TH INNING STRETCH
QUOTES BY JOHN BERNS

"Your most valuable deposits are in your memory bank."

"Be aware that your dreams occasionally include nightmares."

"The grass may be greener on the other side, but there also will be patches of brown over there."

"If I don't tell my story, nobody else will."

"If silence is golden, I might have a shot at the bronze!"

8

7TH INNING - THE UNKNOWN FAN

MY FIRST YEAR AS A HIGH SCHOOL COACH SAW MY 1994 Sevastopol Pioneers start 0-2, including a gut-wrenching 4-3 loss to the Oconto Falls Panthers. On Friday, April 29th we boarded our bus for the eighty-mile ride from downtown Institute to Oconto Falls, seeking revenge for that earlier loss. As I filled in my lineup card, the name of our senior ace, Ryan Tanck, was placed pitching and batting in the number three spot. We were in the midst of a streak that would see our team win eighteen out of twenty games, and I was liking our chances with Ryan on the mound today.

As we arrived at the ballpark in Oconto Falls, the players and managers gathered up our gear and took it to our bench (no dugout). I took one last look down the aisle, on the seats, and on the floor, and headed for the bus door. With my first step off the bus, I was greeted by an elderly fan proudly wearing his Oconto Falls cap. Our conversation was quite brief. He asked, "Is Tanck pitching today?" When I said "Yes," he replied, "Good." Those were the only five words I would hear him speak, but he had spoken volumes with those few words. That veteran fan knew who he wanted to see pitch that day, and he would not be disappointed!

Our guys took a 1-0 lead in the top of the second inning on a hit, stolen base, and two wild pitches. An RBI double in the bottom of the third tied the score 1-1. Sevastopol went back on top 2-1 in the top of the fifth behind a walk, sacrifice, and a throwing error. An insurance run was added in the seventh on a walk and back-to-back singles.

That Oconto Falls fan never moved from his seat directly behind home plate for the entire game. He watched as Ryan Tanck tossed a five-hitter, striking out nine and walking one. A typical Tanck performance, which saw Ryan earn First Team All-Conference honors, finishing

his senior year with a 7-1 pitching record. Although I suspect that fan may have preferred a 1-0 Oconto Falls victory, he had to enjoy the tightly contested 3-1 Sevastopol win.

You can't put a price tag on a knowledgeable fan, as they truly are priceless. I'm sure that gentleman would have enjoyed watching Ryan twirl another five-hitter, in a 3-1 Regional Championship triumph over Reedville later that spring. That performance included thirteen strikeouts. He also would have relished a seat behind home plate during

Tanck's 1-0 gem over Wisconsin Heights in the Sectional Semi-Final. However, I'm certain that this baseball fanatic (fan) knew he was in for a good day at the ballpark when I answered yes to his question, "Is Tanck pitching today?"

YOUR TURN!

1. Describe that fan or two who went to every game and really cared.

_____

_____

_____

_____

_____

_____

2. Memories are wonderful. List some of your fondest memories post high school.

_____

_____

_____

_____

_____

_____

3. Describe a job you have held where you enjoyed the work and the people you worked with.

_____

_____

_____

_____

_____

4. Who are three athletes or leaders that you admire and why?

_____

_____

_____

_____

_____

_____

9

8TH INNING - GORDIE GILLESPIE

THE FIRST TIME I MET GORDIE GILLESPIE WAS AT A COACHING clinic at Ripon College in late winter of 1995. Although Gillespie was just a few months short of his sixty-ninth birthday, he was a striking presence as he bounced all over the gym that day. Gordie had one speed – overdrive!

His energy and enthusiasm kept everybody riveted on each word from his mouth. Whether he was talking skills, drills, strategies, or relating some of his spellbinding stories, everyone stayed fully engaged. He inspired everyone that day, and he made me proud that to a degree, we shared the same profession.

Gordie Gillespie graduated from Kelvyn Park High School in Chicago, Illinois, and enrolled at DePaul University. He played basketball at DePaul under legendary coach Ray

Meyer and toured with the College All-Stars when they played the Harlem Globetrotters.

At age twenty-six, Gillespie began his baseball head coaching career at Lewis University in 1953. After twenty-four years at Lewis, Gordie headed the baseball program at then St. Francis College (IL) from 1977-1995. A persuasive athletic director at Ripon College convinced him to head north for the 1996 season. Athletic Director Bob Gillespie was that persuasive individual, who just happened to be Gordie's son! After a ten year stint at Ripon, Gillespie went back to St. Francis from 2006-2010 to complete a brilliant fifty-eight year career as a head college baseball coach. He had retired with a record of 1,893-952, and in 1998 had been named the NAIA "Coach of the Century" by Collegiate Baseball Magazine.

I was privileged to see Gordie as a clinician at numerous Wisconsin Baseball Coaches Association conventions. He taught me that your catcher was the true team leader, and he needed to have the following personality traits: "Half Ray Nitschke and half Dick Butkus!" Also, to have a successful team, your squad required the following mindset: "Half of your team has to hate losing, and the other half has to love winning!" All of his messages were presented with that unmistakable Gillespie flair. He had a true passion for his life's work, and it oozed out of his pores when he was talking baseball.

The day of the 1995 Ripon clinic I was afforded an opportunity for a brief conversation with this great coach and man.

He was selling his "Baseball Drill Book," and I knew that his book should be in my baseball library. It was a 217 page "bible" including three categories: Defensive Drills, Offensive Drills, and Special Category Drills. His signed note in my book still resonates today:

John,

God bless your work with young people.

Sincerely,

Gordie Gillespie

Time to complete this inning, but not until I share the mission statement from our 2018 Sturgeon Bay High School Baseball Player Handbook. That statement is a quote stolen from Ralph Waldo Emerson:

"Nothing great can be accomplished without enthusiasm"

That quote captures the essence of Gordie Gillespie!

YOUR TURN!

1. Gordie Gillespie's book is in my personal library. List a few books from your personal library and explain why they are important to you.

_____

_____

_____

_____

_____

2. List the three most energetic personalities you have met and how their enthusiasm lit a fire under you.

_____

_____

_____

_____

_____

3. List three of your favorite quotes/sayings.

_____

_____

_____

_____

_____

_____

4. List men and woman in your line of work who taught you techniques or skills that made you better.

_____

_____

_____

_____

_____

_____

10

9TH INNING - DARWIN "DIP" DADE

IT'S THE FIRST SATURDAY OF JUNE IN 1995, AND I'M AT THE Sevastopol Town Park to watch a prep league for 13-year-olds. I'm wearing a Chicago Cubs shirt as I watch some of my future Sevastopol Pioneers do battle, when a man walks over to me wearing a Chicago Cubs cap. He states that he has heard that the local high school team has just qualified for the state tournament in Wausau. I proudly tell him that I am the head coach of that team, and our conversation moves into high gear. That conversation is still active twenty-five years later.

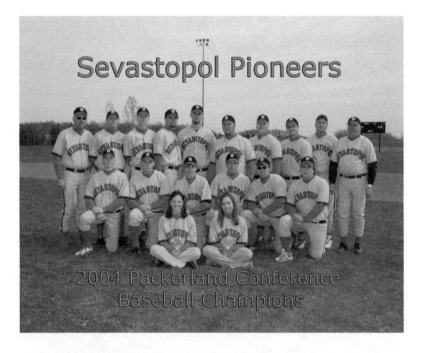

I had just met Darwin "Dip" Dade, a retired teacher from Tomah, WI with a cabin in Jacksonport (Door County). It immediately became clear that we shared a passion for baseball, and before we parted company that day, I offered him a coaching job for the 1996 season. He expressed interest and said we should communicate after the completion of tournament competition.

Dade grew up in Janesville, where he did not have the opportunity to play high school baseball. However, at the tender age of fourteen, he was already coaching a team of twelve-year-olds in that city. After high school graduation he entered the armed services in the last days of World War II. Dade's pitching success for military teams drew the interest of professional scouts. He eventually signed a minor league contract with the Chicago Cubs, where his "sinker" earned him the nickname "Dip" from a Texas sportswriter.

By the time I met Coach Dade, he had already served as either assistant or head baseball coach at Tomah for thirty-one years. Additionally, he had helped raise funds to build and maintain fourteen ball fields for the youth of that community. Because of our chance meeting, this man was about to add a very special nine-year chapter to his already illustrious coaching career.

The Dade and Berns coaching partnership was formed in the spring of 1996. I always gave "Dip" the opportunity to add comments to whatever skills were being taught that day, but being strong-willed and bull-headed, I pretty much did things "my way." However, one day the veteran coach (I was in my third year) looked at me and said, "John, when two people agree on everything, one of those people is unnecessary!" Message received.

From that day forward I became a much better listener when he was making a coaching/teaching point. Our partnership resulted in Packerland Conference Championships for Sevastopol in both 2002 and 2004, the school's first conference baseball titles since 1985. We were very like-minded regarding how to play the game of baseball properly.

Driving between Door County and Tomah each weekend, Coach Dade logged over 50,000 miles in his truck during our nine years together. Those trips were a "labor of love" to be teaching the game he cherished so dearly. While "Dip" was great at teaching various and subtle baseball skills, his greatest skill involved the teaching of qualities such as respect and responsibility. Because of his lifelong contributions to high school baseball, I nominated Coach Dade for the Wisconsin Baseball Coaches Association Hall of Fame in the spring of 2008. He was inducted into the WBCA Hall of Fame, class of 2009.

When the curtain came down on Dade's coaching career, he had already coached at various levels for sixty years. I'm sure his memories of that career could fill a number of very entertaining books. I will most remember our time spent together by his following statement at a baseball game in 2019: "John, the best nine years I had in baseball were our years together at Sevastopol!"

YOUR TURN!

1. Who are some of your lifelong friends and what has kept you together?

_____

_____

_____

_____

_____

_____

2. How did you meet these friends?

_____

_____

_____

_____

_____

_____

3. Who do you know that has gone the extra mile (labor of love) just to help you?

_____

_____

_____

_____

_____

_____

4. Which friends had nicknames and how did they come to be named?

_____

_____

_____

_____

_____

5. List all the cars or trucks you have owned.

_____

_____

_____

_____

_____

_____

11

EXTRA INNING - DAD

John and Dad

MY HIGH SCHOOL GRADUATION CEREMONY WAS HELD IN THE
evening on June 2, 1967. The party to celebrate this momen-

tous occasion involved enough "nonsense" to get me home at 10:30 the following morning.

Both parents met me about ten seconds after I entered the house. Mom expressed her discontent with a

tight-lipped mouth and her head moving from side-to-side. Dad eased the situation by simply looking at me and saying, "Ohhhhh – you're home."

The Berns brothers with Dad at Wrigley Field. L-R, Tom, Dad, Butch, John

Three months later as I was about to enter college, a beautiful song was released. To this day, every time I hear Louis Armstrong sing "What a Wonderful World," I listen intently until the song ends. I have requested that song be played at my funeral. The song is about hope and faith in the world. It allows us to look at bright sides and positive things. We are reminded that this world, although somewhat tarnished, is still filled with love - "Yes, I think to myself, what a wonderful world!"

Yes, it certainly is a wonderful world, when this seventy-one-year-old son can still have a meaningful conversation with his one hundred and two-year-old father! Dad still arranges music and plays the piano daily at Anna's Healthcare in Sturgeon Bay. We certainly have been blessed.

In Mom and Dad's back yard prior to trip to Miller Park.

Time to finish this reflection on my baseball life with a few father-son memories:

1. I will never forget those tennis balls short hopping me in front of the garage door starting in 1957.

2. Our annual trips to Milwaukee County Stadium from 1957-1965.

3. His presence at my Little League games in 1960 and 1961.

4. Seeing our Sevastopol team win a Sectional title in 1995.

5. One week later watching that same team compete in the State Tournament at Wausau.

6. Sitting together to watch the final game played at Milwaukee County Stadium on September 28, 2000.

7. In May of 2002 watching Sevastopol win their first conference championship since 1985.

8. "Having a catch" with Dad at the Field of Dreams in June of 2002.

And the drum roll, please:

9. Knowing how very proud Dad is that his son John is a high school baseball coach.

YOUR TURN!

Whether it is your dad or just memories, list nine other memories not listed that might let the next generation know what you enjoyed and saw as important.

_____

_____

_____

_____

_____

_____

_____

_____

_____

_____

_____

_____

_____

_____

_____

_____

_____

_____

_____

_____

_____

_____

_____

_____

_____

COMPLETING THE ROSTER

WHEN YOU HAVE LIVED IN NINE different decades, you come in contact with many special people who have positively impacted your life. Therefore, I must expand my list of those within my baseball circle of influence.

TOM BERNS

Brother Tom and I have many shared baseball memories. We played together in Little League and high school. Numerous special days were spent together at Milwaukee County Stadium, and recent years have seen us adding to those moments at Miller Park. Reflecting back to our youth makes me nostalgic for those days. More memories will be made. I have greatly benefited from my brother's interest in photography. Tom took over one hundred field level pictures at the State Tournament in 1995, when he talked his way onto the field by convincing tournament officials that he was the official photographer for Sevastopol High School!

Another one hundred images were captured at my final Sevastopol game in 2007. The trifecta was completed by his creation of an amazing two hundred picture flash drive, featuring our Sturgeon Bay Clippers at the Random Lake Sectional in 2019.

Some additional information that allows "Tommy's Trifecta" to be turned into a "Grand Slam" - over 80% of the photos and articles presented in this book were contributed by Dr. Thomas Berns.

Thanks, brother.

DOUG MELVIN

My brother Tom is a close friend of Doug Melvin. In 1996, Melvin received the Sporting News Executive of the Year Award, as general manager of the Texas Rangers. In 2011, as general manager of the Milwaukee Brewers, Doug was named by Baseball America as its Major League Executive of the Year.

In 2012 this native of Chatham, Ontario was inducted into the Canadian Baseball Hall of Fame. He currently serves as the senior special advisor with the Milwaukee Brewers.

I, too, have a special connection to Doug Melvin. When I was inducted into the Door County Baseball Hall of Fame in 2014, Doug penned a special congratulatory letter to be delivered by Tom at the induction ceremony. His perceptive and touching message is presented on the back cover of this book.

That framed letter hangs on the wall in my "man cave" in Sturgeon Bay.

Thanks, Doug.

DARREL SEVERSON

I decided to bench two of my starters for the first game of my high school coaching career for skipping a team meeting the previous day. Their absence directly led to a one run defeat in that game. As I slumped in my recliner prior to calling in results to local media, I received a phone call. That call came from Athletic Director, Darrel Severson.

He praised me for my actions, stating that my decision would pay future dividends, and to "Go get the next one!" What a class act! He made me feel like our team had won that first game. At that moment I knew ours would be a special relationship. It proved to be all of that for the nine years we spent together.

Although Darrel moved out of the athletic director position after the 2002 season, we remain friends. We are part of a Saturday morning "breakfast club," and have dined out with our wives at our sides on numerous occasions.

Thanks, Darrel.

SAM ANDRE

Coach Sam Andre and I were teammates on the 1960 Sturgeon Bay Little League All-Star Team. His diverse skill set allowed him to catch the first game and be our starting pitcher in game two. We also wore the same uniform for grade school football and basketball, American Legion baseball, and various adult fastpitch softball and basketball squads. Sam was always a dedicated team player. Therefore, it came as no surprise when he later transitioned into coaching.

Sam Andre is about to start his thirtieth year as a baseball coach at Sturgeon Bay High School. He has been a valued member of every staff on which he has served. When we both applied for coaching positions at Sturgeon Bay in November of 2017, we had predetermined our roles, if hired. Sam preferred teaching fundamentals at the junior varsity level, and he strongly supported my desire to become the head varsity coach. I will forever be grateful for that support, as both of us were hired for those respective positions in December of 2017.

Thanks, Sam.

TOM ROY

Tom Roy started Unlimited Potential, Inc (UPI) in 1981. The stated core mission of UPI remains to reach, teach, train, and then send out professional baseball players with the gospel message. Tom is now the President of Shepherd Coach Network, and is the acclaimed author of eight inspirational books. I am extremely proud to count Tom Roy as one of my friends.

For many years I had scribbled notes about baseball in various notebooks scattered throughout my home. As the volume of those notes grew, I pondered the idea of organizing my thoughts into some sort of coherent document, never beginning that process. Enter Tom Roy! After discussing my life in baseball, this man of deep faith decided to place his faith in me. It was his belief that these scattered notes might be the genesis (biblical reference intended) of an entertaining book. I moved from originally thinking "Why", to "Why not?"

Throughout this process, Tom has been my mentor. He has supported and encouraged me along the entire journey. Without his incredible skill set and caring nature, the story of my baseball life would remain buried in those notebooks.

Thanks, Tom.

This book would be incomplete wthout a tribute to my late mother, Lucille. The majority of pictures presented in this book were taken by Mom.

She rarely appeared in photos. In fact, many pictures of my mother are of her in the process of taking a picture! Although she passed on February 11, 2011, her positive influence is still present today.

Thanks, Mom.

THIS STURGEON BAY Legion team will carry a 4-1 Fox River Valley League record to unbeaten Marinette Tuesday afternoon. Marinette was rained out Sunday while Sturgeon Bay lost an exhibition game to Fort Atkinson. First row, left to right, Bill Johnson, John Berns, Jim Brauer, Bob Delchambre and Lee Petrina. Second row, Batboy "Rico" Seiler, Chris Larsen, Bill Kroll and Bob Hunsader. Back row, Assistant Manager John Utnehmer, Mark Ostrand, Jon Hanson, John Geitner, Chuck Kroll and Manager George Husby. Steve Ash, Harry Schopf and Mark Honald were not present when the picture was taken.

—Harmann

1967 Sturgeon Bay American Legion team.

Advocate photo by Dan Sollinen

Gibraltar's Justin Hartel awaits a throw, while Sevastopol's Willy Kroll reaches third base safely under the watchful eye of coach John Berns.

Berns named Top pitcher In FVL north

Sturgeon Bay's John Berns was named the Fox River Valley League's top pitcher in the northern division and was also named to the division's all-star team at the annual league banquet at Hollandtown Sunday.

The banquet was attended by about 400 players, coaches, managers, Legion members and other interested people representing the 22 league teams. Attending from Sturgeon Bay were team members Mark Ostrand, John Geitner, Chuck Kroll, Bill Kroll, Harry Schopf and John Berns and manager George Husby, assistant John Utnehmer, and business manager Bill Behringer.

After the meal, trophies were awarded and the all-star teams from each division were named. Berns received the trophy for the top pitcher in the northern division with a 6-2 record. Rick Schwener of Marinette received the trophy for the top batter in the northern division. His average was .446. This is the third year in a row that he won the award. Team trophies were given out to Green Bay West, Northern Division champion; Waupaca, Central Division champion, and Fond du Lac, Southern Division and also League champion. Members of the Fond du Lac team received individual trophies for winning the League championship.

In addition to receiving his trophy for top pitcher in the division, Berns also received an emblem for being named to the division's all-star team.

YOUR TURN!

1. What are some of your favorite memories of an older or younger brother? If you did not have one, mention the fond memories of your best friend.

_____

_____

_____

_____

_____

2. In the course of your lifetime you may have rubbed shoulders with someone who the world saw as important. Let your readers understand how that happened and the value of that relationship.

_____

_____

_____

_____

_____

_____

3. Who are people that encouraged you during your life? Share what you can about how those individuals and their words made a difference.

_____

_____

_____

_____

_____

_____

4. Name and discuss someone who you worked with that just clicked. They made your job interesting and complemented your skill set.

_____

_____

_____

_____

_____

_____

5. Describe for your readers what you would view as your 'spiritual journey' on this planet.

_____

ADDITIONAL PHOTOS

Ron Vandertie and John Berns in Honolulu, Hawaii at the gravesite of the "father of modern baseball," Alexander Joy Cartwright.

Vicky Berns sandwiched between her brothers John and Tom.

L-R, John Berns, Keith Chaudoir, Sam Andre and Jerry Knutson. Keith and Jerry were starting infielders on the 1962 Sturgeon Bay high school team.

Berns holding lineup card delivered to pre-game umpire meeting by 1962 teammates.

Berns, Andre and varsity assistant, Kent Berkley.

Coach Berns and Andrew Carbajal at start of 2019 Sectional Semi-Final.

L-R, Reece Nellis, Coach Berns and Jake Schneider in discussion prior to Nellis' RBI single in a 1-0 Sectional Semi-Final victory.

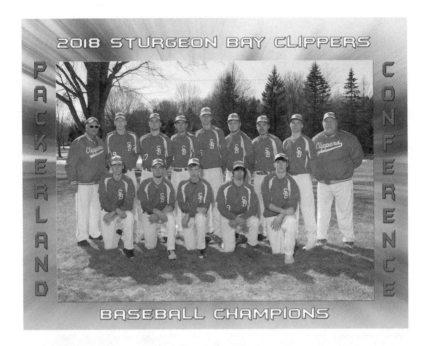

Sevastopol and Sturgeon Bay team pictures courtesy of Photos by Matt, Inc.

JOHN BERNS is a proud lifelong resident of Door County (WI). His thirty-two year career with a local manufacturing company abruptly ended when he discovered the meaning of the word "outsource." Other activities have included twelve years as a high school substitute teacher, and fourteen years umpiring high school baseball and softball. He recently completed his sixteenth season as a trolley tour driver/guide for a local company. Additionally, this spring will find him enjoying his twentieth year as a high school baseball coach, currently serving as the head coach at Sturgeon Bay High School. John was inducted into the Door County Baseball Hall of Fame in 2014. John and his wife, Kris, live in Sturgeon Bay, Wisconsin, and their immediate family includes two children and two grandchildren.

TOM ROY was the founder and president of Unlimited Potential, Inc., a ministry with professional baseball players. He has been a voice in major league baseball for almost four decades. Tom also coached baseball at the high school and college level for eighteen years, and is currently leading *Shepherd Coach Network*. Tom and his wife, Carin, live in Winona Lake, Indiana, and they are the parents of two adult daughters and have six grandchildren.